KT-513-432

BUSY PLACES

Supermarket

Carol Watson

W
FRANKLIN WATTS
NEW YORK • LONDON • SYDNEY

It's 10 o'clock at night and work is just beginning for some of the supermarket staff. At the back door a lorry has arrived with a delivery.

The lorry reverses into an open door at the back of the supermarket building. The night workers unload the boxes and take them into the store, ready to fill the shelves.

Inside the store the Day Duty Manager is 'handing over' to the Night Duty Manager. He tells him about the important things that have happened during the day.

Meanwhile the night workers start to fill the shelves. They look to see where there are only a few things left and make sure they put out plenty more.

"That should be enough yoghurt," thinks John.

Other staff are checking and changing the price labels.

One of them uses a small computer which tells him if the supplies are running out.

At 3 o'clock in the morning
the bakers begin work.
First they make the bread.
Later, when the loaves
come out of the oven,
they wrap them up
ready to be sold.

At 6 a.m. more staff arrive to put out the fresh meat and fish. They scrub the counters clean before they display the food.
Some of the fish is on special offer today.

"Time to load the chickens," says Chris. She puts the chickens into the oven to cook and they turn slowly round and round.

Later, when the customers arrive, the chickens will be golden brown.

While the chickens are cooking the staff at the delicatessen counter prepare the cheese and cold meats. One of them uses a large machine to slice some ham.

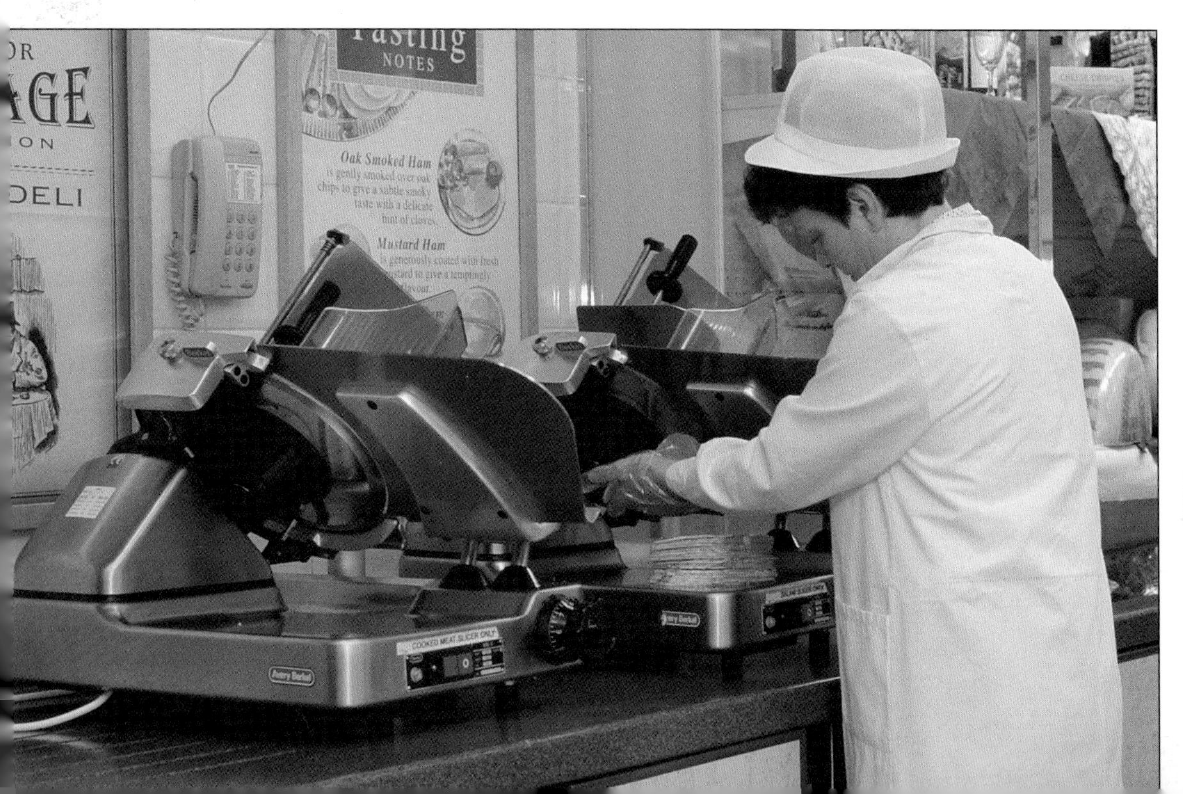

Meanwhile the day's newspapers and magazines have just arrived.
An assistant puts them neatly on display ready for people to buy.

All around the store the cleaners are busy too. They clean and polish the floors and collect the rubbish.

At the front of the supermarket, other staff are preparing the cash desks. The Controller puts money into the tills ready for the Customer Assistants.

Peter puts out plenty of carrier bags for the customers to use.

Now everything is ready
for the Customer Assistants to take up
their positions at the checkouts.
The shelves are neatly stacked and the
store is clean and tidy.

It's opening time!
The customers start to arrive.
They collect a trolley
or a basket near the
entrance to the supermarket.

Soon the store is very busy.
People search the shelves
for all the things they want to buy.
"Where is the milk?" one woman says to herself.

Some of the trolleys have seats
for small children. These twins are
looking after the shopping
while their mum collects more fruit.

Sometimes customers stop to eat at the café inside the store.
"Can I have another drink, Mum?" asks one child.

The Receptionist speaks into the microphone. "Will Mrs Jones please go to the Customer Reception Desk where her little boy Ben is waiting," she says.

Outside Peter is collecting trolleys from the car park.

At the till a Checkout Operator puts the bar code from each item close to a scanner.

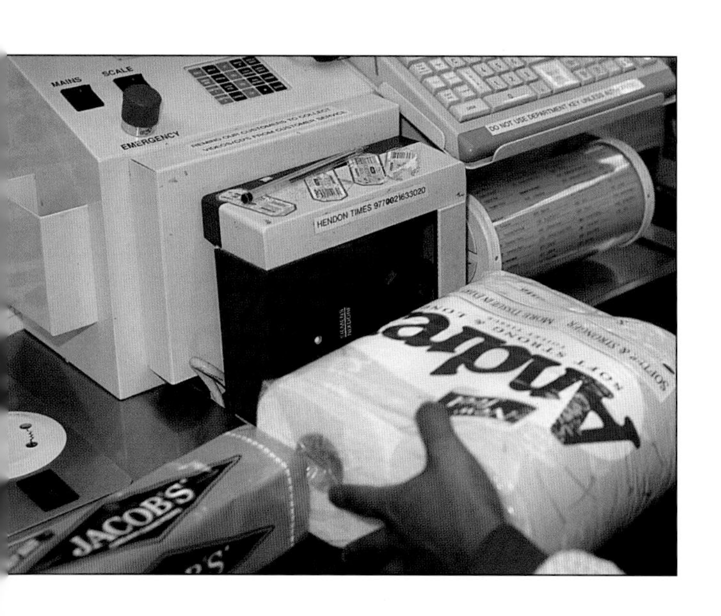

This reads the price and shows it on the display. The machine adds up how much the customer has spent.

"Can I help you pack your shopping?" asks a Customer Assistant.
She puts the shopping into carrier bags while the customer pays the bill.

When they have bought everything they need, the customers leave the supermarket. It's time to take all the shopping home.

Care and safety in a supermarket

When you are in a busy supermarket, it is important to make sure you and others keep safe.

Try to remember some of these tips:

1. Always keep close to your parent or friend.
2. If you get lost, find a member of the supermarket staff.
3. Make sure toddlers keep their hands inside the trolley so other shoppers don't bump into them.
4. If you spill something, tell someone who works in the supermarket. They will call the janitor who will clean up the mess so that no-one slips and hurts themselves.

Index

96 Leonard Street
London
EC2A 4RH

Franklin Watts Australia
14 Mars Road
Lane Cove
NSW 2066

ISBN 0 7496 2795 6

Dewey Decimal Classification Number
381

A CIP catalogue record for this book is available from the British Library

Printed in Hong Kong.

Editor: Samantha Armstrong
Designer: Kirstie Billingham
Photographer: Harry Cory-Wright
Illustrations: Kim Woolley

With thanks to all the staff at
Tesco Supermarket, Brent Cross.

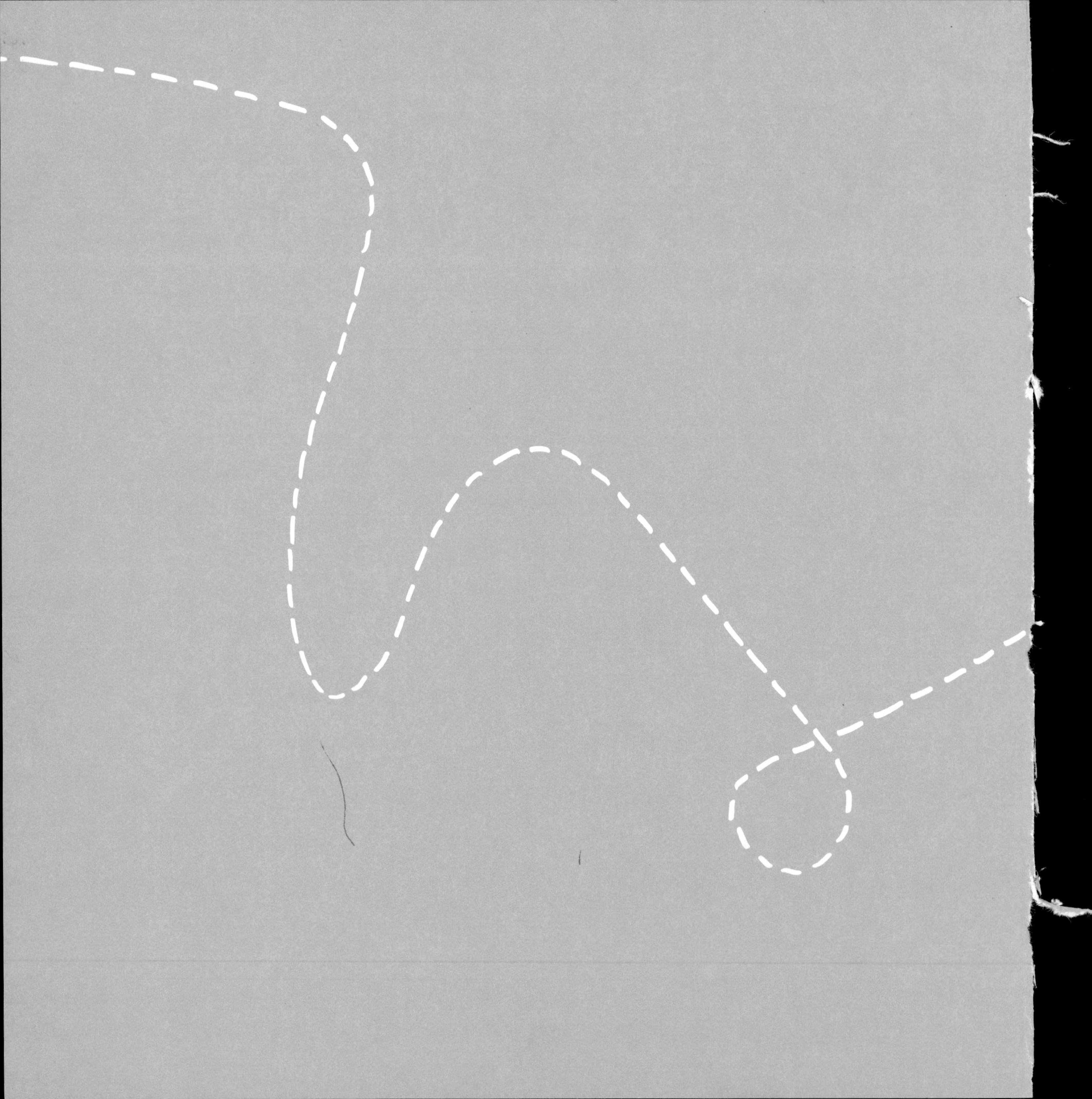